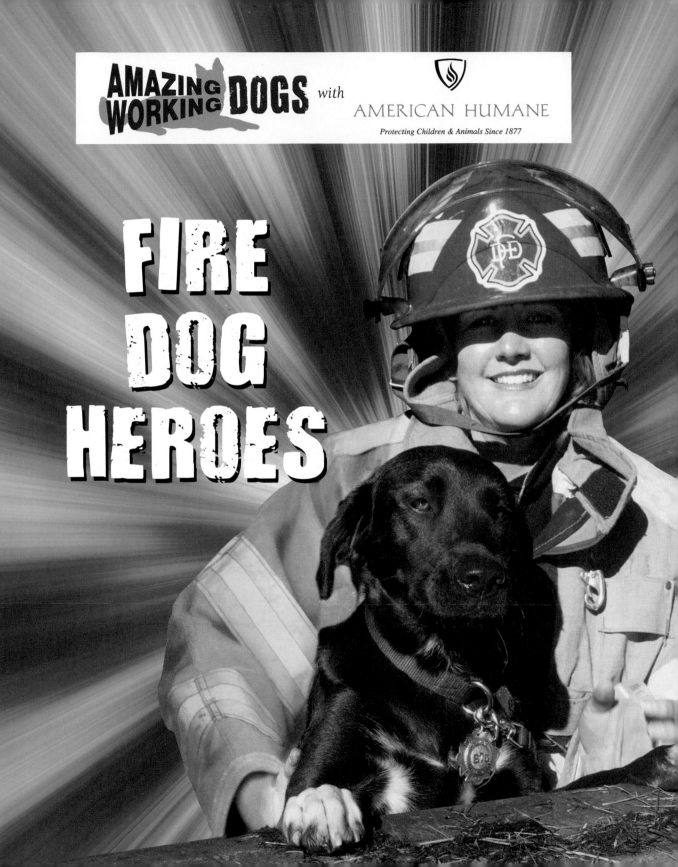

Titles in the Amazing Working Dogs with American Humane Series

FIRE DOG HEROES
ISBN-13: 978-0-7660-3202-6

GUIDE DOG HEROES
ISBN-13: 978-0-7660-3198-2

POLICE DOG HEROES
ISBN-13: 978-0-7660-3197-5

SEARCH AND RESCUE DOG HEROES
ISBN-13: 978-0-7660-3201-9

SERVICE DOG HEROES
ISBN-13: 978-0-7660-3199-9

THERAPY DOG HEROES
ISBN-13: 978-0-7660-3200-2

AMAZING WORKING DOGS *with*

AMERICAN HUMANE
Protecting Children & Animals Since 1877

FIRE DOG HEROES

Linda
Bozzo

Bailey Books
an imprint of
Enslow Publishers, Inc.
40 Industrial Road
Box 398
Berkeley Heights, NJ 07922
USA
http://www.enslow.com

This book is dedicated to Debra Mullins and her K-9 Ashly for sharing their story.

Founded in 1877, the American Humane Association is the only national organization dedicated to protecting both children and animals. Through a network of child and animal protection agencies and individuals, American Humane develops policies, legislation, curricula, and training programs—and takes action—to protect children and animals from abuse, neglect, and exploitation. To learn how you can support American Humane's vision of a nation where no child or animal will ever be a victim of abuse or neglect, visit www.americanhumane.org, phone (303) 792-9900, or write to the American Humane Association at 63 Inverness Drive East, Englewood, Colorado, 80112-5117.

AMERICAN HUMANE

Protecting Children & Animals Since 1877

Bailey Books, an imprint of Enslow Publishers, Inc.

Library of Congress Cataloging-in-Publication Data

Bozzo, Linda.

    Fire dog heroes / Linda Bozzo.

       p. cm. — (Amazing working dogs with American Humane)

    Includes bibliographical references and index.

    Summary: "The text opens with a true story of an arson dog, and then it explains the history of the arson K-9 team and the training methods used to transform an ordinary dog into a canine hero"—Provided by publisher.

    ISBN-13: 978-0-7660-3202-6

    ISBN-10: 0-7660-3202-7

    1. Firehouse dogs—Juvenile literature. 2. Detector dogs—Juvenile literature. 3. Arson investigation—Juvenile literature. 4. Dogs—Training—Juvenile literature. I. Title.

    TH9148.B69 2010

    636.7'0886—dc22

                           2008048019

Printed in China

052010 Leo Paper Group, Heshan City, Guangdong, China.

10 9 8 7 6 5 4 3 2 1

To Our Readers: We have done our best to make sure all Internet Addresses in this book were active and appropriate when we went to press. However, the author and the publisher have no control over and assume no liability for the material available on those Internet sites or on other Web sites they may link to. Any comments or suggestions can be sent by e-mail to comments@enslow.com or to the address on the back cover.

Every effort has been made to locate all copyright holders of material used in this book. If any errors or omissions have occurred, corrections will be made in future editions of this book.

Illustration Credits: Associated Press, pp. 34, 36, 37, 40; © Bettmann/Corbis, p. 14; Courtesy of James Butterworth, pp. 18–19, 20; Dallas Fire-Rescue photographer Jon Freilich (Freilich Creative Services), pp. 1, 3, 8, 13; Masterfile, p. 42; D.L. Mullins, p. 11; Courtesy of Seattle Fire Department, p. 44; Shutterstock, pp. 6, 22, 24; Photo provided by State Farm Insurance®, pp. 26, 27, 29, 31; Time & Life Pictures/Getty Images, p. 16.

Cover Illustration: Dallas Fire-Rescue photographer Jon Freilich (Freilich Creative Services).

Contents

Thank You

Enslow Publishers, Inc. wishes to thank James Culpepper, Co-owner of Lead K-9 and Vice President of the American Working Dog Association for reviewing this book.

The author would like to thank Jim Butterworth and Doug Lancelot for sharing their memories of Mattie. She would also like to thank Charles (Bucky) Simpson, and her good friend Frank Sacco for all of their help.

What's in a name?

The proper name for fire dogs is accelerant detection dogs. These dogs detect accelerants, or liquids that help start or spread a fire. Sometimes, fire dogs are also called arson dogs because they help convict people of setting a fire on purpose, a crime called arson. Many people simply call them fire dogs. Throughout this book, these working dogs are called fire dogs.

Ashly
A True Story

A fast-moving fire burns through an apartment building. The first floor of one unit suffers heavy fire damage. There is reason to believe the fire was set on purpose. Debra Mullins, fire investigator with the Dallas Fire Department, and Ashly, her fire dog, are called into action. Fire dogs are trained to quickly find accelerants such as gasoline and paint thinner. Accelerants, often liquids, are used to start or spread fires. Accelerants are often used in arson.

Ashly sniffs around debris trying to find an accelerant.

The next day, after the area has had a chance to cool, Debra and Ashly arrive anxious to work their first fire scene together. Ashly wears a special badge attached to her collar. This badge tells people that Ashly is a working dog. On her leash, Ashly sits at the front door of the apartment. She waits patiently for

Debra to give a command. It is determined that the scene is safe. The search can begin. Debra commands Ashly to "go find."

Ashly wastes no time. Excited to go to work, she runs into the apartment. She enters the living room where investigators think the fire may have started. Ashly lowers her nose to the ground and sniffs. Then she lifts her nose and sniffs the air. Within seconds, Ashly "catches," or detects, an odor. She follows it into the kitchen where she sits in the middle of the floor. Ashly stares at the spot. This is how she "alerts" Debra, or lets Debra know that she has found something.

Ashly is sitting amid a pile of food spilled from the overturned refrigerator. For a moment, Debra wonders if Ashly is focused on the food odors or if she actually found an accelerant odor. "The most important thing they teach you in all the weeks of training is to trust your dog!" says Debra. She marks the spot and takes pictures of the mess. Debra then begins to remove the food and fallen ceiling tiles. That is when she discovers burn marks on the kitchen floor. The burn pattern Debra sees usually indicates that an accelerant was poured there.

Ashly made her first find. Debra praises Ashly. "Good girl, Ashly. Very good girl!" She pats Ashly on her side and rubs her favorite spot, her ears. Debra takes a treat from her pocket. It is Ashly's reward for her alert. That day stands out in Debra's mind. "Ashly showed that all the months of training and hard work had paid off."

Debra collects samples of Ashly's find for testing. She and Ashly continue their search. In the dining room, Ashly sits again, this time in the corner among a pile of melted trash and a trash can. Debra sifts through the mess on the floor. She is not surprised

Ashly sits in the Dallas Fire-Rescue vehicle.

when she finds another accelerant, a can of charcoal lighter fluid. She wonders if the lighter fluid could just be from the family's barbecue.

Investigators will have to conduct an interview and wait for test results. The laboratory will check to see if the charcoal lighter fluid matches the accelerant poured on the kitchen floor. For now, Ashly has done her job.

As Debra removes the can from the trash, Ashly's ears perk up. She looks at the staircase leading to the second floor. Ashly lets out a whine. Debra knows she is trying to tell her something. She gives the command, "Go find." Ashly bounds up the stairs while Debra follows close behind. When they reach the top, Ashly rushes into a bedroom. She pokes her head in the open closet door, her tail sticking out and wagging wildly. Debra peers in. Behind a pile of boxes, she spies a kitten, shivering with fright.

"Well, Ashly," Debra says, "you might not be a trained rescue dog, but I guess it is a natural instinct." She scoops the kitten up into her arms so it can be returned to the family.

The investigation into the cause of the fire continued. As first thought, the fire was not an accident. Thanks to Ashly, investigators were able to gather enough evidence as to the cause of the fire. The man responsible was arrested for pouring an accelerant and setting it on fire.

Since that day, Ashly has worked on hundreds of fires. "She attends many events and activities in the community," Debra says. "She is a valued member of the Fire Department. At home, Ashly loves to roam the large piece of land she lives on with her friend, a black Lab named Pepper, and the family cats, goats, and horses."

More About Ashly

Ashly is a Labrador retriever and Border collie mix. Found abandoned, she was rescued by two members of the Dallas Fire Department. Shortly after, Ashly was adopted by her handler, Debra Mullins.

Ashly and Debra Mullins

In the early 1940s, these Dalmatians were brought to the scene of a fire. They have first aid kits strapped to their backs.

Chapter 1

The History of Fire Dogs

ogs have worked with fire companies since the 1700s. Back then, horses pulled fire trucks called steam pumpers. Dalmatian dogs kept the horses company in their stables. Dogs also helped keep the horses calm during fires. A dog's role in fire service today is quite different.

Early in the 1980s, the possibility of dogs being trained to sniff for accelerants the same way they were trained to sniff for bombs was just an idea. But in

In the early
1940s, this
firefighter
trained a
Dalmatian
as a fire dog.

1984, it was a retired New York police officer who experimented with the idea. He worked with his own dog, a yellow Labrador retriever named Nellie. He trained Nellie to find the odor of gasoline, an accelerant. That same year, Nellie was introduced to the Connecticut State Police. They were amazed by what she could do.

In May of 1986, the Guide Dog Foundation donated a black Labrador retriever named Mattie to the Connecticut State Police. Their efforts were combined with the U.S. Bureau of Alcohol, Tobacco

ATF

Effective January 24, 2003, the Bureau of Alcohol, Tobacco and Firearms (ATF) changed its name to the Bureau of Alcohol, Tobacco, Firearms and Explosives (ATF) and its law enforcement functions were transferred from the Treasury Department to the Department of Justice.

and Firearms to start the first accelerant detector dog program.

Three instructors from the Connecticut State Police Canine Training Center were assigned to train Mattie. "We used a food reward system and a specially prepared gasoline," explains one of Mattie's trainers, Jim Butterworth. Not only did they train Mattie to sniff odors,

Mattie was the first fire dog!

they trained her to find these odors on fire scenes. "The dog basically learned from making mistakes and repeating tasks until she got it right," says Jim.

Less than a month later, Mattie worked on her first fire scene with Jim. She worked from June until September that year in the New Haven, Connecticut, area. Mattie was so successful in finding accelerants that in September they began using her across the state of Connecticut. "We waited to make sure what we were doing with Mattie worked before we spread the word," Jim says.

In 1989, they told the world of Mattie's success. The Connecticut State Police began offering seminars

Mattie was given a special award.

on fire dogs with the ATF. In June 1990, Jim accepted
another position. Doug Lancelot took over the care of
Mattie. Mattie, the world's first arson dog, retired with
Doug in 1997.

"Over her career Mattie traveled across the United
States," Doug says.

"She was on more than four hundred fire scenes. She had an accuracy rate of over 80 percent," Jim adds.

Today, fire dogs and their handlers, known as K-9 teams, are located throughout the United States. These working dogs help fire departments, law enforcement agencies, and even insurance companies with arson investigations.

The History of Fire Prevention Week

On October 9, 1911, Fire Prevention Day was proclaimed. This day was chosen because it was the fortieth anniversary of the 1871 Great Chicago Fire, which killed hundreds of people and destroyed thousands of buildings. In 1992, Fire Prevention Day was extended to an entire week. Fire Prevention Week is celebrated during the week that includes the date of October 9.

Labrador retrievers are just one breed of dog that can make a good fire dog.

Chapter 2

Fire Dog Breeds

Most fire dog programs prefer to train Labrador retrievers for arson work. This breed has an excellent sense of smell. This allows them to find accelerants in less time than humans can. Labrador retrievers are known to be social dogs. This means they get along well with people. This is important for arson work. Fire dogs work closely with their handlers and other fire investigators. Labrador retrievers are known to be eager to please their handlers. This makes them easy to train for arson work. They must learn to obey commands from their handlers.

Fire dogs must have a strong desire to work. Labrador retrievers are known for their willingness to work. These are just a few reasons why this breed is preferred when training fire dogs. Other breeds that are sometimes trained are golden retrievers, Labrador mixes, golden mixes, and German shepherds.

Golden retrievers also make good fire dogs.

Chapter 3

Arson K-9 Team Training

Fire dogs provide a great service to investigators. These dogs have to be properly trained to perform accelerant detection work.

Fire dogs and the people who handle them are called an arson K-9 team. They work together to train in accelerant detection. It is the trainer's job to prepare the arson K-9 team for accelerant detection. The arson K-9 team may also provide educational programs to their community.

Fire Dog Handlers

A fire dog handler is the person who owns or is assigned the dog by a department. The handler trains along with the fire dog. It is the handler who is responsible for the care of his or her dog.

Fire dogs and their handlers are called an arson K-9 team.

Fire Dogs

Dogs are taught by a trainer to recognize accelerant odors. Paint thinner, gasoline, and charcoal lighter fluid are just a few examples of accelerants.

The U.S. Bureau of Alcohol, Tobacco, Firearms and Explosives train its dogs on leads, or attached to leashes. This helps the handlers to keep their dogs safe from debris, like nails or glass. Being on a lead also helps to keep a dog from eating things that could be dangerous.

Some fire dogs are trained using playtime as a reward. Most fire dogs are trained using food as a reward. The trainer will allow the dog to sniff a small

This dog is being trained to sniff for accelerants.

amount of a specially prepared accelerant. The dog then receives a small amount of food. This trains the dog to make the connection between the smell of the accelerant and food. Additional accelerants are introduced using a food-reward or play-reward system.

The dog is taught to act in a certain way when he finds an accelerant. The dog may sit or place his nose in a certain spot. This is how the dog tells the handler that he has found something. This is called an "alert." Fire dogs must learn not to disturb the spot so the handler can collect a sample for testing.

Fire dogs are also trained to move quickly and easily so they can work around different obstacles like walls or stairs. Fire dogs are trained to work in different environments. Fire scenes might include places like factories, warehouses, or people's homes. These dogs must learn how to work on different surfaces, such as fire debris, gravel, and grass.

Fire dogs are also trained to move quickly and easily. The dogs and their handlers move their way through an obstacle course.

Fire dogs train to work on fire scenes that contain other odors, such as food, without being distracted. During training, if the dog takes an interest in an odor other than an accelerant, the dog is not rewarded.

Fire dogs need to know some basic commands such as "sit" and "find." They are also taught to detect accelerants on different types of material, including wood and clothing. For example, Jim Butterworth remembers a time when investigators were questioning a property owner about a fire. Jim and Mattie happened to be walking by. "Without being commanded, Mattie's nose went straight to the owner's shoes. She alerted me that she had found an accelerant."

Fire dogs must also train to work on actual fire scenes. They must get used to the sights, sounds, and smells of fire scenes before they are tested.

Most fire dogs need to pass tests before they can be called fire dogs.

Passing the Test

To become an arson K-9 team, the handler and dog need to pass a series of tests. These tests measure the ability of the fire dog and the handler. Once they have passed, the arson K-9 team can begin their work. When used properly, fire dogs aid in arsonists being convicted of their crime, which is starting a fire on purpose.

Training never ends as long as the fire dog and handler are working together. They continue to train and retest throughout their career.

Chapter 4

Fire Dogs on the Job

The arson K-9 team is called when there is reason to believe an accelerant may have been used to start a fire. It is the dog's job to help find it. The nose knows! These dog detectives help investigators track down and arrest people who commit arson.

The fire dog's job begins when he arrives on the scene. The fire has burned out and the area has had

Fire dogs and their handlers are called to a scene of a fire. Fire dogs can sniff for things that may have started the fire, such as gasoline.

a chance to cool. The scene is cleared for safety before the dog can begin searching. It is time to go to work!

How Fire Dogs Work

The dog is given a command such as "find" to start her search. Dogs can smell the smallest traces of accelerants while humans or machines cannot. They also work faster than humans. This saves investigators time.

If the fire dog smells, or catches, an odor, she will give an alert. The dog's behavior will change. Each dog has her own way of telling her handler that she has found something. "Our dogs show us exactly where the sample should be taken by placing their noses in the location of the accelerant," Bucky Simpson with the ATF explains.

The spot is marked. Samples are taken from any spots the dog has alerted. The samples are sent to a laboratory, or lab. A properly trained dog will cut

Fire dogs keep training until they retire.

down on the number of accelerant samples taken. This helps save money. The lab will test the samples to determine what type of accelerant was found. Lab results are used in court to convict arsonists of setting a fire on purpose.

Fire dogs not only search fire scenes for accelerants, they may perform field searches. This means searching for evidence that the arsonist may have tried to hide. A person's vehicle is also often searched for evidence by the dog. Fire dogs can be used to sniff clothing or other samples that may have been removed from a fire scene.

These firefighters are bringing a fire dog to the scene of a fire.

Fire dogs are rewarded after each of their finds. These dogs are rewarded with food or playtime with a favorite toy. They also enjoy plenty of praise for a job well done. No wonder these dogs love their jobs!

When they are not at work, most dogs live at home with their handlers. They are part of the handler's family. The only difference is that these pets have a job. Sniffing out accelerants is hard work. Fire dogs are always on call and ready to help.

Chapter 5

When Fire Dogs Retire

Just like people, fire dogs retire too. It is time for a fire dog to retire when he can no longer do his job. This can be due to an injury or illness. In some cases, the dog may no longer be able to pass the certification test. The first arson dog, Mattie, retired because her handler, Doug Lancelot, retired.

When a fire dog retires, it means that the dog no longer works fire scenes. In most cases, after the dog retires, like Mattie, she will live with her handler.

Wendt was a fire dog in Charlotte, North Carolina. The dog was given a special retirement ceremony in 2004.

After all, they have both spent many hours together at home and at work.

Just like any pet, a fire dog is part of the family. The powerful bond between dog and handler does not end when the fire dog retires. These hardworking dogs make excellent pets. They are loving and well trained. It may take some time for a retired dog to get used to retired life. After all, the dog is used to being busy working and training.

While the fire dog's working days may be over, his life with his handler is not. Together they will continue to enjoy each other's company in a loving home. What a perfect reward for these hardworking dogs.

Once a fire dog is retired, he can be adopted by his handler or a loving family.

Chapter 6

Fire Dogs Are Heroes

A hero is said to be "one that shows great courage." Without a question, fire dogs are heroes. Day after day, these dogs risk their lives working on or around fire scenes. These astonishing animals work in communities all over the country. They seem to love the work they do. Each year, property is damaged and lives are lost as a result of fires set by arsonists. That is where the help of fire dogs comes in.

These everyday heroes help investigators gather evidence. Finding traces of accelerants takes skill. It could be searching a burned-out building or a suspect's vehicle for evidence. This evidence helps convict arsonists of their crime. Fire dogs are crime-fighting heroes!

Fire dogs are true heroes!

Glossary

accelerants—Certain materials used to start or spread a fire.

alert—The way a fire dog lets the handler know that he or she has found something.

arson—The crime of starting a fire on purpose.

arsonists—People who commit the crime of arson.

breed—A certain type of dog.

convict—To find guilty.

debris—What is left of something broken down or destroyed.

evidence—Material that is presented in court.

investigator—A person who closely studies the cause of a fire.

laboratory—A place where tests are done.

obstacle—Something that stands in the way.

on lead—Attached to a leash.

Further Reading

Jackson, Donna M. *Hero Dogs: Courageous Canines in Action*. New York: Little, Brown, 2003.

Latham, Donna. *Fire Dogs*. New York: Bearport Publishing, 2006.

Miller, Marie-Therese. *Distinguished Dogs*. New York: Chelsea Clubhouse, 2007.

O'Sullivan, Robyn. *More Than Man's Best Friend: The Story of Working Dogs*. Washington, D.C.: National Geographic, 2006.

Internet Addresses

American Humane Association
  www.americanhumane.org

New York State Department of State Fire Safety
  for Kids: Arson Dogs
  www.dos.state.ny.us/kidsroom/firesafe/adogs.html

U.S. Fire Administration for Kids
  usfa.dhs.gov/kids/flash.shtm

Index